IN THE MIDST

MIDST

Spoken Word and Poems

JOYCE BLACKMON

WestBow Press books may be ordered through booksellers or by contacting:

WestBow Press
A Division of Thomas Nelson & Zondervan
1663 Liberty Drive
Bloomington, IN 47403
www.westbowpress.com
1 (866) 928-1240

ISBN: 978-1-9736-9090-0 (sc)
ISBN: 978-1-9736-9091-7 (e)

Library of Congress Control Number: 2020907725

Print information available on the last page.

WestBow Press rev. date: 06/01/2020

WESTBOW
PRESS®
A DIVISION OF THOMAS NELSON
& ZONDERVAN

IN THE MIDST

CONTENTS

DEDICATION

To my husband Darryl Blackmon, thank you for understanding my past, accepting that I have a past and loving me for the woman that I am today.

For those reasons and many more I am dedicating these words and this book to you.

I love you and I appreciate you!!!

INTRODUCTION

We all have a story, some parts of that story we want to share and some parts we prefer to keep deep inside until we depart from this side. Well, a part of my life story is, some of the words, thoughts and feelings that are shared in this book.

In the midst of certain situations and circumstances I have spoken about that moment, some moments more intimate than others but still in the midst.

Everything is not always perfect or pretty but when things are good I strongly believe just as much attention should be given to the good things in life as we give to the negative. With that being said, I hope whoever reads this enjoys a little of my good and is able to reflect on your good, even if it's that one time you can recall that left a smile on your face….In the midst.

He Doesn't Have To Do It.

He doesn't have to just sit there and listen,

He doesn't have to give insight to any part of my life,

He doesn't have to make sure I have a little cash in my pocket,

BUT......

He Loves me, this man really loves me and because of that, the wonderful gift that God has given me,

He does just sit there and listen,

He does give insight to any part of my life,

He does make sure I have a little cash in my pocket,

No, he doesn't have to but he does and because he does, I do too...

Just sit there and listen,

Give insight to any part of his life,

And yes ....I ask if he has a little cash in his pocket,

I don't have to do it.....Love does it...

This Thing

It has been said that Coca-Cola is the real thing, but this thing, this feeling, these butterflies in the pit of my stomach, this thing I cannot put into words. It feels better than what has been called the real thing yet I can't figure it out, what to call this thing.

It feels like love beyond the word love itself; it feels like a peace that passes all understanding.

WAIT, it's not a thing it's you; it's your spirit dwelling in me where the Holy Spirit is dwelling. This thing is love beyond words, it is a peace that passes all understanding...it's you….so good had to say it twice, this thing..

This together, handsome, intelligent, noble, God-fearing man, it's you!!

Thank you for this thing!!

Making Love With Your Clothes On

This man makes love to me with our intellectual conversation,

This man makes love to me by holding my hand sitting on the couch,

O my just when I didn't think it could get any better, now we begin to talk about the lyrics of real music, you know that old school Donny Hathaway, Steve Wonder, L.T.D., music while at the same time listening to the fireplace crackle as the background.

….I look over as he speaking, and this man is fine to me!!!!

A smile just comes over me; we continue the conversation into the early morning hours of the night,

….Sports, Religion, Politics, Education, the conversation is warm, inviting, interesting a real turn on, something to be considered a real turn on

Every fiber of my mental capacity has just been massaged,

I am sleepy now….he takes me, lays me down, kiss on the check, I love you, he lays beside me with…good night….I have just been made love to with my clothes on……

YOUR WIFE

I cannot and will not speak for other women about what they think a wife is or should be, BUT as your wife…

I promise to be more than physical, more than emotional, more than your chef…

I WILL BE YOUR PRAYER WARRIOR….

….through prayer anything is possible, which means this marriage IS successful, we are joined together as one and no one or nothing can break that bond.

….we are healthy and yes, we are wealthy, and we will have and do what we are blessed and gifted to do, in the name of Jesus. I love you and thank you for giving me the gift and honor of being called YOUR WIFE!!!!!

ALL OF IT

So we are not intimate....medical reasons maybe, just tired, I don't think so....
nope, I got it, he thinks I am FAT...wow....very difficult to continue in this thing
called marriage. Am I perfect, OF COURSE NOT!! Do I try UMMM YEA!!!
but at this point...for what....I truly try and satisfy just because I love him. Yes,
I do work, pay bills, cook, do laundry and keep a clean house, but for what...the
bottom line is he is simply not turned on and that's an issue I am a person that
enjoys every possible kind of intimacy and I am truly unsatisfied. No cooking, rare
cleaning, no laundry and no regular climatic moments, no soft music, no flowers,
no cards, no candy and I am fat...Jesus I need you to stay in this and be true,
this is not the marriage I wanted or hoped for...maybe he feels the same way....
Just another ploy by the devil to destroy a marriage in the middle of a dry
moment!!!! Our minds or should I say my mind goes alllll the way to the left..
...deep breath, pray, God, I give All Of It to you, whew, that was close, this too
shall pass!!

When A Military Man Sleeps

I have found that when my military man slept, soundly and peacefully in my arms what a compliment and a moment to treasure. That is a trust that, that man had bestowed on me that should not and was not ever broken.

Even if a military man has not gone to war, the training he went through and goes through is war within himself. He is now trained to always be on guard for any and everything, even in his subconscious…WOW!!!

You mean there is no solidarity in the one thing that this military man needs most to rejuvenate himself; real rest.

So when my military man slept, I felt as though it is my duty to give that man the peace that is due him, and know that the trust that has been bestowed on me is a beautiful blessing…..When a military man sleeps.

WHAT HAVE YOU DONE FOR ME LATELY?

A song that we all know so well, but really is in need of an answer. What have you done for me lately?....

Well, let me explain what you have done for me lately, you have made me smile; harder and longer than I ever have before; you have given me the inspiration to want to succeed again; you have made love to me to the point of tears and in that vulnerable open moment you gave me the security of, "it's ok.", by holding me and kissing those tears away.

These are just a few things of what you have you done for me lately, an area where money has no amount and emotion has no limit.

I can only pray that what you have done for me lately, I am able to return to you with, as much surety and sincerity.

What a powerful question when it comes from a place of pure gratitude...What have you done for me lately?

Sleepless

I toss and I turn only to return to the thoughts of you and I, us.

I'm tossing and I'm and turning now becoming torn with the past thoughts of you and I, us.

Sleepless….

Now I am wishing, wishing thoughts of you and I, us, as I toss and turn hoping and praying that this sleepless moment will pass…wait… the phone rings, only to hear that you too are sleepless; you too have been tossing, turning, wishing, hoping and praying..

Now tears streaming, the past we are not, torn we may be yet repairable…a simple miscommunication to a powerful, I am sorry…

Sleeping now, never to be sleepless again, well at least for tonight..

Fuss, Fight, Figure It Out!!

Why are there so many breakups and divorces today? One among many issues are we fuss, fight, and FLEE....What happen to the good ole days of fussing, fighting, and figuring it out to stay together…but let's digress for just a moment, I am not saying fussing and fighting and figuring it out when there is abuse in the midst, the reference is to fussing and fighting and figuring it out over things, such as did you have to cut your hair, or why can't you just pick up behind yourself like a normal person…wait. One more, one more, how about can you simply close your mouth while chewing…get the picture.

Now that we get the picture, there is that space between fighting and figuring it out, it is cooling and praying. The cooling and praying is the true staying power missing in our culture today. I want to return to the days of ole, if there is a point to be heard; I want the freedom of fussing and fighting without the fear of fleeing; the twist to that strength comes from the fussing and fighting to get to the praying and cooling, so you know what to do to figure it out, to now be that blessing to someone else that is trying to figure it out.

In the short a quick teaching of ole, the staying power, to the strength to the fuss, to the fight and figure it out would be a family that prays together, stays together…words to be treasured by the days of ole…

Consideration Shown

He has been in and out of meetings all day, on and off the phone conference call after conference call, yet in the midst of it all he considers the woman he loves…babe do you need or want anything before I get home…wow what a man. Not once speaking or complaining about the day, but in that moment only considering mine..

Consideration, hmmmmmmm, what a word to consider; what a man to live up to such a word not used often enough……..this man is:

Charming

Offering

Never Judging

Sexy

Intuitive

Determined

Endearing

Respectful

Aspiring

Tenacious

Insightful

Needed and necessary in my life,

How I love this considerate man, showing such consideration for the woman he loves.

Real Love is Work....
Is It Worth It?

Love is work, true work, a conscious or an unconscious decision, love is work. Work to sustain, work to want it, and work to stay in love; just work, another 9 to 5, 24/7 job and it is the best NEVER paid job in existence. Love has an ultimate payout, beyond lust and any other 2 second fulfillment ever thought of or created. Yes, real arguments ensue, yes, we get on each other's very last and reserved nerve from time to time that make you question, why on earth are we even doing this thing, but "LOVE."

So to answer is it worth it, YES! Love lets you know, no matter what 110% I, We, You are not going anywhere and we gotta work.

Why is it worth it, what's the payout with no pay? Knowing someone has your back through it all, having that person to laugh with, talk to, pray with, pray for, play with, take care of; be taken care of, going to dinner with, watching the game with, listening to music with, going to the movies with, waking up in the morning with bad breath, saying good morning, thanking the Lord he allowed another day with this person, to love on again. What a mercy granted to love a person and be loved by a person.

Real Love is work and worth it!!

You Give Me Reason...Purpose, Drive and Determination

The reason to get up in the morning, the reason to know that I am depended upon,

The purpose to know why I have been placed on this earth, and give clarity to the calling that God has placed on my life,

The drive, because let's face it, sometimes the purpose and calling can be a challenge, worth it, but a challenge,

The determination because I am blessed to be a blessing, so if I am not doing what I am supposed to be doing, yes determined, how will that person that is to be blessed by my hand get their blessing. That is the equivalent of having blood on your hands.

Being faithful to God is the reason, purpose, drive and determination to live this life.

IT'S THOSE

To every woman, those 'it's those' might be different, but no matter what those 'it's those' are we as women, especially African American Woman, that have strong African American men need to make sure that our men know that we notice and appreciate those 'it's those.'

What is an 'it's those', it's that thing or those things that he does without a thank you.

For me, I am emotional during that time of the month and he recognizes it, so I get those extra hugs, those extra intense kisses, those words, "babe. I appreciate you." It's those, vacuuming the on the weekend, just so I can sit a little while longer, it's that, him washing dishes without me saying a word because I just made a serious 7 course meal after I just got off of work, it's that let me drive your car, so we can pull up to a gas station and he fills the tank. Those are 'it's those' and again they may be different for everyone, but whatever they are acknowledge them and him and continue to give him the love that he wants and deserves so those 'it those' continue....now; that's a give and take relationship.

Thank You and Acknowledgements

Thank you Jesus, for allowing me to know if it wasn't for your Grace and Mercy I would surely have lost my mind a long time ago.

Thank you husband, Darryl Blackmon, for simply being my husband and answered prayer.

No matter what I do, always thank you to the three most beautiful people and joys of my life, Britni and Brandi, my daughters that I birthed and my 3rd daughter Maya that because of marriage I have the joy to call mine, they are the reasons to keep going and pushing through life's journey.

Thank you to the mainstays of my life, My mom, Joyce, posthumously, My dad, John Sr., My sister, Janeen, and my brother, John Jr. True meanings of what family is all about; up, down, good, or bad, always having a sista's back.

Thank you Kevin Richardson, for giving me words of encouragement to just do what I need to do and accomplish whatever it is I want to accomplish.

Gabriel Baawo, you said get it done, and I thank you for that!!!

My Cherie, My Tandria, My Michelle, My Gina, My Keisha, My Shaherra, My Camay and My Ricci; True sisterhood, so blessed for my beautiful inspirational friends during this time of my life, Thank You!!

Printed in the United States
By Bookmasters